REBEL GIRLS
ANIMAL ALLIES

25 TALES OF WOMEN WORKING WITH WILDLIFE

www.rebelgirls.com

Some of the artwork in this book has been previously published in the book *Good Night Stories for Rebel Girls.*

Text by Sofía Aguilar, Sarah Parvis, and Shelbi Polk
Art direction by Giulia Flamini
Foreword by Lucy King
Activities by Wildlife Warriors
Cover illustrations by Annalisa Ventura
Graphic design by Kristen Brittain
Special thanks: Amy Pfister, Darren Gertler, Eliza Kirby, Grace Srinivasiah, Hannah Fox, Jess Harriton, Kate Berry, Maithy Vu, Marina Asenjo, Michon Vanderpoel

Library of Congress Control Number: 2022942678
Rebel Girls, Inc.
421 Elm Ave.
Larkspur, CA 94939

Printed in China, 2022
10 9 8 7 6 5 4 3 2 1
ISBN: 978-1-953424-42-6

FSC
www.fsc.org
MIX
Paper from
responsible sources
FSC® C169965

CONTENTS

FOREWORD

Dear Rebels,

I was brought up surrounded by animals. As a child, I befriended two giant Somali spurred tortoises that roamed around in our tangled garden in Mogadishu. I also lived on a farm in Lesotho, where my family and I had the chance to explore the extraordinary wild corners of southern Africa. I always felt pulled to protect and stick up for the special animals that made my young world so interesting and colorful.

I must have been about five years old, bouncing down a sandy game park track on safari in our old Ford Cortina, when my father slammed on the brakes. The car skidded to a halt, and he switched off the engine. Elephants. They slowly meandered around the car. From my lowly position in the back seat, I squished my nose against the window and stared up at four towering pillars to a wrinkly gray underbelly. The elephants loomed over the top of our car. Their presence and sheer size awed me, but it was their quiet, chest-shaking rumbles as they ate that captured my heart. I have been completely, head over heels in love with elephants ever since. I would do anything to protect them and have, actually—I've ended up in the hospital several times from the rough-and-tumble of life working with elephants.

I can see the same passion in the women featured in this book, like Rachel Ikemeh, who has been striving to safeguard red colobus monkeys in her home country of Nigeria, or Leela Hazzah, who works with Maasai warriors to protect lions in Kenya. Hana Ahmed Raza has lobbied for protected areas to keep the last few Persian leopards from disappearing from Iraq. Like these passionate conservationists, I have been compelled by my lifelong interest in elephants and my rising awareness of their changing and disappearing habitats to help elephants and humans live in better harmony. It's simply impossible for me to imagine the African landscape without elephants.

By listening to Kenyan herders who live with wild animals every day, my team and I at Save the Elephants learned that these giant pachyderms are afraid of honeybees. Yup—incredible, isn't it? This led my team and I to develop a novel "beehive fence" to keep elephants from raiding farms for crops. Our beehives are hung between posts and interlinked so they swing and release the bees if an elephant tries to push through. By first exploring and understanding the natural behaviors of both elephants and bees, we have created a sustainable solution that benefits both species. It also protects some of the poorest farmers from elephant conflict.

I hope that our story of working with animals, not against them, plus this wonderful compilation of tales about astoundingly fearless Rebel Girls, will encourage you to embrace your instincts to protect an animal that captures your heart. Do anything to defend it. Whether that means helping a local rescue shelter, planting flowers for pollinators, rehabilitating injured creatures, or tracking wild mammals across the plains of Africa, we all need to do our part to protect and nurture our fellow earthly species of all shapes and sizes. I don't think there is anything more important—after all, our very lives depend on the health and vitality that animals contribute to our shared planet.

—Lucy King, Head of Human-Elephant Co-Existence Program
Save the Elephants, Kenya

SCAN TO
HEAR MORE!

BONUS! AUDIO STORIES!

Download the Rebel Girls app to hear longer stories about some of the dedicated planet protectors in this book. You will also unlock creative activities and discover stories of other trailblazing women. Whenever you come across a bookmark icon, scan the code, and you'll be whisked away on an audio adventure.

AMANDA VINCENT
AND HEATHER KOLDEWEY

MARINE BIOLOGISTS

With a scuba tank on her back and goggles protecting her eyes, Amanda leaned back. Out of the boat she splashed. And into the water she went. There, underwater, she got to work doing something no other biologist was doing: studying seahorses in their habitat.

Amanda watched these quirky little fish wrap their wriggly tails around seagrasses and corals to stay put in the constantly shifting shallow waters. Such interesting little creatures! They use their snouts to suck up food as it floats by. And when it comes to babies, it is the males who give birth.

Seahorses were a joy to study, but Amanda knew they were also in trouble. They get trapped in fishing nets and caught by people who use dried seahorses in traditional medicine. Like a detective, she tracked the trade in seahorses. Amanda also met a powerful partner, Heather.

Heather had planned to be a veterinarian. But the tides pulled her in another direction, and she became a marine biologist. She too wanted to save the seahorses. So Amanda and Heather combined forces.

They needed to learn more about how fishing communities relied on the seahorse trade. Soon the devoted scientists were in the Philippines, balanced in a boat in the middle of the night with a seahorse fisher.

Amanda and Heather founded Project Seahorse to bring people together to protect marine ecosystems. They got seahorses added to an important worldwide list of endangered species. And now 183 nations (and counting!) are working toward a sustainable seahorse trade. When oceans are safe for seahorses, it's better for all sea creatures—and humans too!

AMANDA, BIRTH DATE UNKNOWN
HEATHER, BORN JANUARY 18, 1967
CANADA AND UNITED KINGDOM

"IT'S NOT JUST BIOLOGISTS AND SHOULDN'T BE—EVERYONE CAN BE A CONSERVATIONIST."
—HEATHER KOLDEWEY

ILLUSTRATION BY JOJO CLINCH

BELLA LACK

ENVIRONMENTAL ACTIVIST

Bella flopped on the sofa. Her eyes were wide, and she was ready to learn. Images of animals in the wild darted across the TV screen, and a deep voice rose over the outdoor images. She'd recognize that voice anywhere. It was Sir David Attenborough, and she loved the wildlife documentaries he made. She grabbed a pen and wrote him a letter.

Something incredible happened. David wrote back. Every time. His replies made Bella feel like her words mattered.

As a young girl, Bella learned about animals that performed in circuses all over the United Kingdom. Many lived in tiny cages and faced brutal training. She couldn't stand it.

At first, Bella felt small. Circuses had been around forever, and she was just a teenager. But then Bella remembered the letters that had brought her so much joy. What if she wrote a letter to lawmakers?

Bella sat down at her computer and started writing. She imagined she was talking to someone like Sir David Attenborough and expressed how much she cared about the bears, tigers, elephants, and other four-legged entertainers. She begged the government to outlaw their acts.

Later she turned her letter into an online petition and asked her friends for help spreading the word. They shared it with their friends, who shared it with their friends. Bella was blown away when 200,000 people signed it!

Less than a year later, a new law passed. It banned the use of animals in circuses in the UK. Bella is more convinced than ever that her words matter. She proved that no one is too small or too young to speak up when something is wrong.

BORN NOVEMBER 27, 2002
UNITED KINGDOM

ILLUSTRATION BY
EMMA PEDERSEN

"THERE'S NO
WAY WE CAN GET
PEOPLE TO CARE
ABOUT NATURE
IF THEY DON'T
KNOW WHAT
THEY'RE TRYING
TO PROTECT."
—BELLA LACK

BINDI IRWIN

TV PERSONALITY
AND CONSERVATIONIST

indi wasn't born in the Australia Zoo, but she might as well have been. The enormous wildlife sanctuary has always been her home. Every animal inside it is like family to her. She was even named after her father's favorite crocodile! While at the zoo, Bindi would run from habitat to habitat, feeding koalas, kangaroos, snakes, and turtles right from her hand and memorizing the name of every new joey, pup, and hatchling. She squealed as she played with her best friend, Maggie, a magpie goose.

Bindi's father, Steve Irwin, was a famous conservationist with his very own TV show. One day, she wanted to be just like her adventure-loving dad. Sure enough, when Bindi turned seven, she began filming her own show, *Bindi, The Jungle Girl*. In it, she and her family introduced audiences to koalas, kangaroos, macaws, and more. She showed off lizards in the outback, spotted prairie dogs in the American West, and fed grapes to her iguana at home. Two years later, she won an Emmy Award for the show!

Sadly, when Bindi was eight years old, her dad passed away while filming a nature documentary. Though Bindi was heartbroken, she was also determined to continue his legacy.

Bindi has worked as an educator, tour guide, and animal caretaker at the zoo—feeding and caring for the animals (including her most beloved wild friends, echidnas!). While teaching children worldwide about the importance of preserving wildlife, she is raising her own daughter in the same incredible, enriching home where she grew up. Bindi hopes that the next generation will love animals as much as her family, and that her dad's enthusiasm for the whole wild world—and her own—will never be forgotten.

BORN JULY 24, 1998
AUSTRALIA

"FROM THE MOMENT I WAS BORN, MY WONDERFUL MUM AND DAD STARTED INTRODUCING ME TO WILDLIFE. OUR CONSERVATION WORK HAS BEEN MY LIFE SINCE THE VERY BEGINNING." —BINDI IRWIN

ILLUSTRATION BY JOANNE DERTILI

BIRUTÉ GALDIKAS

PRIMATOLOGIST

Biruté found her favorite type of animal in the first book she ever checked out of the library: *Curious George*.

She fell in love with all monkeys and apes. Chimpanzees, bonobos, gorillas—they all captured her attention. But one type of ape stood out: orangutans. When she looked at pictures of them, Biruté saw intelligence. *Are they as curious as I am?* she wondered.

When she got older, Biruté moved to Borneo, a giant island in southeast Asia, where wild orangutans roamed. She followed the animals for years, researching and learning more about orangutans than anyone else on the planet.

All that knowledge made her the perfect person to call when an orphaned orangutan needed help. Conservation officials handed Biruté the small orange creature, and she couldn't help but laugh. This was it. She was holding a baby ape just like Curious George! The orangutan wrapped his tiny hand around her finger when she fed him from a baby bottle.

Biruté taught him how to survive in the wild. She caught him when he tumbled out of trees as he started to climb and swing. She showed him how to pick ripe fruit. She encouraged his curiosity and helped him learn how to stay safe in the jungle. It was a sad day when he was finally ready to leave her side, but Biruté was proud. And she wasn't lonely for long. Soon, there was another orphaned orangutan who needed her.

When Biruté had her own son, his playmates were fuzzy baby orangutans. In nearly 50 years of research, Biruté has sent more than 500 little apes back out to the wild where they belong.

BORN MAY 10, 1946
CANADA

12

"THERE IS NO SEPARATION BETWEEN OURSELVES AND NATURE."
—BIRUTÉ GALDIKAS

ILLUSTRATION BY LAURA PROIETTI

CHRISTINA GORSUCH

ZOO CURATOR

Christina started working in zoos when she was in college. Her career took her all over the US. She tended to rhinos, elephants, giraffes, kangaroos, and other animals. When she landed a job at the Cincinnati Zoo, she met two very special hippos named Henry and Bibi. Christina didn't know it yet, but together the three of them would make history.

Introducing hippos to one another is tricky. It requires lots of planning and coordination. With Christina's assistance, Henry and Bibi began to live together happily. Soon, Bibi was pregnant! Zoo scientists were able to capture an ultrasound image of the calf growing inside her. When they heard the heartbeat, the group gasped. It was the first-ever ultrasound of a Nile hippo. Everyone was excited to meet Bibi and Henry's baby.

Over the next few weeks, Christina monitored Bibi's progress. But things didn't go as planned. The calf arrived six weeks early. She was just 29 pounds. Most newborn hippos weigh 100 pounds—10 times more than a cat! No one knew if she would live to see the next morning.

Christina and her team sprang into action. By analyzing Bibi's milk, they created a special formula to bottle-feed the baby hippo. They gave her oxygen and kept her skin moist. She grew and grew. Christina felt that it was time to give the growing girl a name. Her team looked at the hippo's sweet face. *Didn't her ears look a bit like the ogre's ears in the movie* Shrek? they mused with a laugh. And so they named the baby Fiona, after the film's fair princess.

When Fiona reached about 200 pounds, she began living with her giant parents full-time. Thanks to the dedication of Christina and her team, visitors from all over the world can visit a healthy, happy hippo named Fiona.

BORN JANUARY 8, 1978

UNITED STATES OF AMERICA

"SHE WAS TINY AND FRAGILE
AND JUST PURE ENERGY, AND
IT WAS LOVE AND DEDICATION
THAT GOT HER HERE."
—CHRISTINA GORSUCH

ILLUSTRATION BY
IZZY EVANS

CORINA NEWSOME

ORNITHOLOGIST

The first time Corina saw a blue jay, she shouted—right in the middle of her ornithology class. The bird was just so beautiful! Corina had never noticed blue jays before, but after that class, she began to pay attention to all the birds around her.

With binoculars around her neck, Corina would wander along shady trails and watch flashes of blue or black wings among the leaves overhead. She was so fascinated by birds that she decided to dedicate her career to watching and researching them.

As a graduate student, Corina spent her days creeping through marshes to find seaside sparrow nests—tiny camouflaged nests perched in tall grass. She watched carefully for the bright yellow markings just above their beaks that sparrows are known for. Corina adored her job and the birding community. So when she saw an upsetting story about a Black birder on the news, her heart sank. A white woman in New York City had falsely accused the birder of threatening her in Central Park. Corina knew this would make other Black birders feel unsafe doing the hobby they loved.

On a group chat with about 100 nature lovers, Corina and others discussed the incident. They wanted to show people what an amazing network there was in the birding world and inspire white allies to stand up for Black birders.

On Twitter, Corina and other co-organizers announced the first-ever Black Birders Week! Soon, Black people from all over the world were posting selfies, discussing their research, and organizing nature walks together. Corina was thrilled to see a global community ready to keep one another safe. And she hopes to inspire other girls like her to spread their wings.

BORN APRIL 3, 1993
UNITED STATES OF AMERICA

"DIVERSITY IS IMPORTANT FOR THE ROBUSTNESS OF ANY COMMUNITY TRYING TO DO ANYTHING."
—CORINA NEWSOME

ILLUSTRATION BY
DÉBORA ISLAS

CRISTINA MITTERMEIER

PHOTOGRAPHER AND MARINE BIOLOGIST

Growing up in Mexico, in the sun-drenched state of Morelos, Cristina always admired nature. The ocean enchanted her—the way it frothed with every wave, alive with movement and sound. When she grew up, she became a marine biologist.

Working along the southern coast of Mexico, she saw how the rise of hotels and resorts could be devastating for sea turtles. She adored sea turtles—how they hatched from their soft white shells and used their flippers to scuttle to their new lives in the water. But they needed undisturbed places to nest, hatch, and scuttle. And they needed humans to stand up for them.

Cristina spent a year learning about these magnificent reptiles. She began leading tourists to study their nests in the sand and educating people about ways to safeguard their colonies.

As a scientist, she conducted research, compiled data, and wrote articles. But her scientific papers didn't move people's hearts.

One day, Cristina borrowed a camera from a friend. She aimed the camera, peered through the lens, and *click!* She uncovered a new talent.

Back to school she went.

She learned more about her craft and embraced her new mission: taking photos that would convince people to protect the oceans. A sperm whale unfurling its tail in the sunset, fish darting through a towering kelp forest, a manta ray gliding beneath a tangle of plastic waste—her photos showed the beauty of ocean life and the pollution threatening it.

"Together," she says, "we can turn the tide for our oceans." With photography, she captures unforgettable images—and moves people's hearts.

BORN NOVEMBER 26, 1966

MEXICO

"ANIMALS ARE NOT JUST IMPORTANT TO ME BECAUSE THEY ARE BEAUTIFUL AND BECAUSE THEY MAKE THIS PLANET THE MAGICAL PLACE IT IS, BUT BECAUSE THEY ARE THE NUTS AND BOLTS THAT KEEP SPACESHIP EARTH ALIVE."
—CRISTINA MITTERMEIER

ILLUSTRATION BY
NATALIA CARDONA PUERTA

EUGENIE CLARK

ICHTHYOLOGIST

Eugenie never understood why people were afraid of sharks. Every Saturday, while her mom was at work, she rushed to the New York Aquarium and pressed her face up against the glass of the shark tanks. The sharks' constant, smooth motion ignited her imagination. *What would it be like to swim with them in the ocean?*

Whenever Eugenie had to do a project in school, she knew what subject to pick: marine biology. Book reports, science presentations . . . all led to the ocean. No one in her life was surprised when she decided to become an ichthyologist, a fish scientist.

Eugenie was working at a research lab in Florida when another scientist asked if she could catch a shark for them to study. She teamed up with a fisher, and they pulled it off! Eugenie saw intelligence in the shark's eyes. She rubbed its sandpapery skin and watched it chase fish in the lab. *There's got to be more to these animals than everyone thinks*, Eugenie said to herself.

Many people thought sharks were mindless eating machines, but Eugenie knew better. She designed some experiments to explore their behavior. In one experiment, she even trained wild sharks to do tasks. The sharks learned that they could get treats from her if they pushed a certain button on an underwater target—like big, swimming dogs.

Just as she did as a schoolgirl, Eugenie kept sharing what she learned. She wrote so many books and articles about her research that she earned the nickname Shark Lady! Eugenie dove with sharks until she was 92 years old, and never once did she come out with a bite.

MAY 4, 1922–FEBRUARY 25, 2015
UNITED STATES OF AMERICA

"THE SEA SHOULD BE ENJOYED, AND THE ANIMALS IN IT. WHEN YOU SEE A SHARK UNDERWATER, YOU SHOULD SAY HOW LUCKY I AM TO SEE THIS BEAUTIFUL ANIMAL IN HIS ENVIRONMENT."
—EUGENIE CLARK

ILLUSTRATION BY
BARBARA DZIADOSZ

GILLIAN BURKE

TV PRODUCER,
PRESENTER, AND BIOLOGIST

Gillian was happiest when she was barefoot. Growing up in Kenya, she would climb trees and rocks to see the big world in a new way, even when she got thorns stuck in her legs and feet. She'd crouch down to watch termites build their trails, beetles stretch their wings, and butterflies and sunbirds drink sweet flower nectar.

When she wasn't drawing pictures of her discoveries in her notebook, she was recording her voice. With her mom's tape recorder in hand, she'd pretend to be a TV presenter and narrate the wonders around her. *The bee is landing in the flower bud*, she might've said. *A snake is slithering through the grass*. Then she'd listen to her fake newscaster voice and laugh so hard that she'd roll around on the ground.

When Gillian was old enough, she went to school to study biology so she could learn all about plants and animals—and all natural life.

Armed with a degree and her love of wildlife, she embarked on her career. For 15 years, Gillian worked behind the camera. She traveled the world researching, writing, directing, and learning everything she could about filmmaking. She never thought that one day she'd be a TV presenter—no one on TV looked like her!

But every so often, she would host a radio program. All of that practice as a child paid off. Listeners loved the sound of her voice, and soon she was invited to appear onscreen. As a presenter for Animal Planet, Discovery Channel, the BBC, and others, Gillian has visited six continents and taught people about birds, rabbits, snakes, and more. Gillian no longer listens to her voice alone. Now millions of viewers hear it too.

BORN MARCH 12, 1974
KENYA AND UNITED KINGDOM

"TO ME, EVERY SPECIES IS FASCINATING.... THERE'S ALWAYS A RICH VEIN OF STORIES TO BE TOLD."
—GILLIAN BURKE

ILLUSTRATION BY MONIQUE STEELE

GUNJAN MENON

FILMMAKER

Once there was a girl who dreamed that she lived deep in the forest and gathered stories from every animal she met. Gunjan wanted to protect them and tell their tales to the whole world.

When Gunjan grew up, she decided to do just that. She picked up a camera and headed out into the Himalayas. There, she battled bad weather, treacherous terrain, and blood-sucking leeches in search of one of her favorite animals: the red panda. Gunjan had never seen a red panda in person before, but she would do whatever it took to find and film a wild one.

Gunjan met up with Menuka, a young woman called a Forest Guardian who makes sure no poachers come into the jungle. Gunjan stayed in Menuka's house, and every few days, the pair got up early to walk four hours into the mountains. The long hikes were so tiring that Gunjan almost went home. But who else would tell the story of these charming creatures?

While they were at Menuka's house one day, Gunjan got the call. Another Forest Guardian had spotted a red panda! Gunjan and her team scrambled to gather their gear. They started running. Gunjan was so excited that she made the four-hour hike in half the time.

"The first time I saw a red panda, that was such a magical moment. Nothing compares to seeing a panda in the wild," Gunjan said.

Gunjan wanted to scream with joy, but she kept quiet and crouched low in the underbrush. The red panda looked straight into her eyes, and Gunjan smiled. She had the perfect footage for her film.

Through filmmaking, she and her team can share stories of amazing animals and the people who protect them—just like she always dreamed.

BORN DECEMBER 27, 1992

INDIA

ILLUSTRATION BY
JUNE TIEN

"NATURE WILL SURVIVE EVEN
WITHOUT US. IT WILL BOUNCE
BACK. BUT WE HUMANS DON'T
STAND A CHANCE WITHOUT IT."
—GUNJAN MENON

HANA AHMED RAZA

CONSERVATIONIST

Hana's home in the mountains of Iraqi Kurdistan was alive with the brightest greens in the world. Trees, shrubs, bushes, grasses, and leaves stood out against the soft brown of the rugged peaks. This was her family's safe place, a refuge from the rest of the country.

After studying biology in college, Hana returned to these same mountains to research mammals. She went from village to village asking the locals what animals they saw. Their answer was depressing: "None." Logging, forest fires, wars, hunting, and farming had pushed wildlife from the region. Locals might catch a glimpse of a jackal or a fox.

How about the Persian leopard? Hana would ask.

Yellow and white with black spots and a long tail, the Persian leopard had been important in the local food chain. Leopards still lived in Iran, but no one knew if there were any on the Iraqi side of the mountains. Many believed they had gone extinct in the area, like the Asiatic lion and the cheetah.

The area wasn't very safe for scientists. There were land mines in the ground, left over from wars, that might explode. And some people didn't like conservationists wandering onto their land.

Hana was determined to look for the leopards anyway. She was 24 years old when set up a hidden camera along a trail. Two months later, a colleague flipped through the photos, and Hana was in for a wonderful surprise. She'd done it! She'd captured a shot of a rare Persian leopard on camera.

Hana has never seen the elusive Persian leopard with her own eyes—and that's okay. With the protected areas she's creating, they'll be free to roam, hunt, grow, and thrive, away from humans.

BORN APRIL 28, 1987

IRAQ

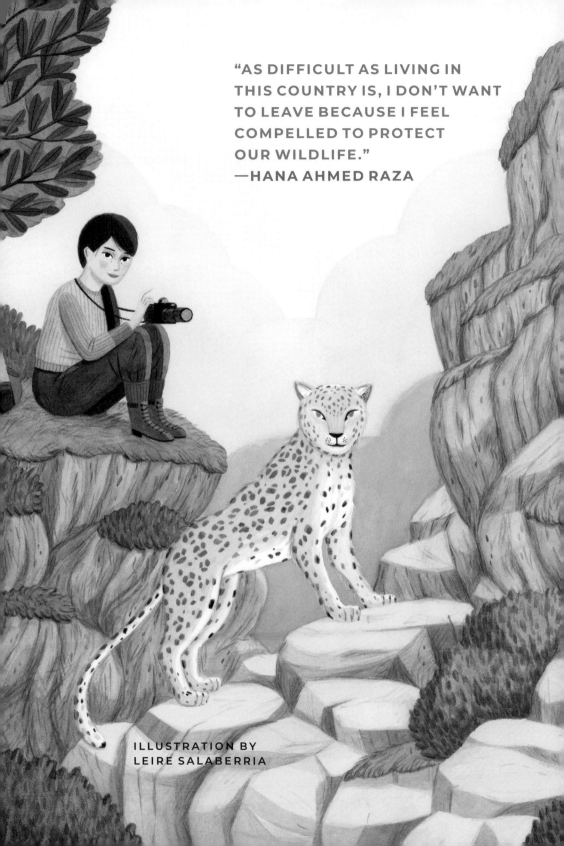

"AS DIFFICULT AS LIVING IN THIS COUNTRY IS, I DON'T WANT TO LEAVE BECAUSE I FEEL COMPELLED TO PROTECT OUR WILDLIFE."
—HANA AHMED RAZA

ILLUSTRATION BY LEIRE SALABERRIA

SCAN TO
HEAR MORE!

JANE GOODALL

PRIMATOLOGIST

Once there was a girl who loved her stuffed chimpanzee more than any other toy. Jubilee the chimpanzee was almost as big as Jane, but she carried him everywhere. When she grew up, Jane had a great idea: she'd become a scientist and study real-life chimpanzees.

When Jane started her research, most scientists studied animals in zoos or sanctuaries. It was odd for a researcher to seek out the animals in the wild. It was even odder for a young woman who'd never even gone to college to move to a foreign country to spend time with apes. But Jane didn't care. She packed her notebook and binoculars and headed off to Tanzania to learn from the experts: the chimps themselves!

Jane realized that the chimps had so much to teach her. She got to know each animal's personality and even gave them funny names like Frodo, Gigi, and Goliath. Eventually, they let her join their group.

Other scientists thought that only people used tools. But one day, Jane saw one of her chimp friends pulling the leaves off a stick. He ambled over to a big termite mound, poked the stick in, and pulled it out covered in termites. Jane knew this wasn't an accident. This chimpanzee had made a tool to get a bite of his favorite snack. Yum!

Everyone needs to know how smart chimpanzees are, Jane thought. So she wrote books and gave lectures all over the world. People were stunned to learn all this new information about her endangered friends.

Not only did Jane change the way humans understand their closest animal relatives, she changed the way scientists study and protect animals. And Jubilee still sits on her dresser today.

BORN APRIL 3, 1934
UNITED KINGDOM

"WHAT YOU DO MAKES A DIFFERENCE, AND YOU HAVE TO DECIDE WHAT KIND OF DIFFERENCE YOU WANT TO MAKE."
—JANE GOODALL

ILLUSTRATION BY EMMANUELLE WALKER

JULIE RAZAFIMANAHAKA

CONSERVATION BIOLOGIST

Off the southeastern coast of Africa is a giant island called Madagascar. It is filled with dazzling, sprawling forests and many animals that aren't found anywhere else on Earth.

Julie loved traveling around her country. When she was 13, she visited one of Madagascar's many national parks with a group of campers. She peered up into the trees, studied insects on her walks, and listened to the chirps and trills of nearby animals. Then, one night, she heard it.

AOOOOH!

It was the call of the indri lemur, an animal found only in Madagascar. First, Julie heard one, then another, then another! *AOOOOH!* they howled. Their calls sounded like a whale song, bigger and louder than Julie would have expected from such small creatures. Her heart pounded.

Julie got her degree and began a career as a bat researcher. But she never forgot the enchanting call of the indris. There were only a few thousand indris left in the whole world. And bats and indris weren't the only endangered animals in Madagascar. Species of chameleons, geckos, snails, frogs, fish, and birds were all threatened. When forests are cut down and people hunt or trade wild animals, populations decline. Plants like the baobab tree were at risk too. She had to take action.

As the leader of a conservation organization, Julie studies endangered species, writes papers about her findings, and works with local communities to save their wildlife and combat climate change. With dedication and communication, she knows the forests of Madagascar can be protected, so the *AOOOOH!* of the indris never falls silent.

BIRTH DATE UNKNOWN
MADAGASCAR

"WITH ANY CHANGE COMES THE OPPORTUNITY TO MAKE PEOPLE REALIZE THAT ANYTHING IS POSSIBLE."
—JULIE RAZAFIMANAHAKA

ILLUSTRATION BY SHIANE SALABIE

KRISTEN BELL

ACTOR AND ANIMAL
RIGHTS ACTIVIST

SCAN TO
HEAR MORE!

From the time Kristen was a kid, she knew she loved two things: acting and animals. Appearing on camera made her feel special, and so did cuddling with dogs and cats. *But if she loved snuggling animals so much, how could she eat them?* she wondered. When she turned 11, she became a vegetarian, which meant she didn't eat meat. Goodbye, burgers. Bring on the brussels sprouts!

When Kristen grew up, she began adopting dogs of her own. There was Sadie, who survived Hurricane Katrina, and Lola, who once took on a coyote who crept into the yard. Pat preferred to nap, and Barbara was a brown-and-black terrier with one eye and a wet nose. Kristen adored her sweet pups.

When Barbara passed away, Kristen was very sad. She missed her furry friend, and she knew what to do.

Kristen went to her local animal shelter. All kinds of dogs sat in the cages—pugs, retrievers, huskies, bulldogs. There were hardly any puppies. Instead, older dogs with sleepy faces and white streaks in their fur looked up at her. Older dogs aren't adopted as often because many people think puppies are cuter. But Kristen likes to spoil senior dogs.

She has adopted many rescue dogs—some old, others with injuries or special needs. One of her dogs, Whiskey, lost a leg in an accident but now lives a healthy, happy life with Kristen and her family. "Adopt, don't shop" is one of Kristen's mantras. An advocate for shelter pets and senior dogs, she posts on her social media, encouraging her followers and friends to adopt animals from local shelters too. Kristen—and Sadie, Lola, and the rest—remind everyone that dogs of any age and ability can be wonderful new friends.

BORN JULY 18, 1980
UNITED STATES OF AMERICA

"I DESPERATELY
WANT TO PROMOTE
HAPPINESS AND
REDUCE SUFFERING."
—KRISTEN BELL

ILLUSTRATION BY
KRISTEN BRITTAIN

KRISTEN LEAR

CONSERVATIONIST AND SCIENCE COMMUNICATOR

Once there was a girl whose Girl Scout project changed her life. When she was 12, Kristen learned how to design and build big rectangular boxes to hang on trees. These simple wooden boxes are homes for bats! Some people think bats are spooky. But Kristen knows the truth. Bats are pollinators. They help new flowers grow, and they eats tons and tons of mosquitoes.

Kristen's favorite kind of bats, long-nosed bats, eat the nectar of a spiky plant called agave. When she started studying long-nosed bats, Kristen discovered that there isn't always enough food on their migration route between Texas and Mexico. So she decided to ask farmers who lived along the bats' long flight path if she could help them plant agave.

The first time she knocked on a stranger's door, Kristen thought, *What if they laugh at me? What if they don't care about bats?* Still, Kristen wiped her sweaty palms on her pants, took a deep breath, and tapped on that door in sunny south Texas.

To her delight, Kristen found that lots of farmers were willing to help! Whenever someone agrees to plant agave, Kristen makes sure to work alongside them to find areas with enough room for the plant's 15-foot-tall flowers to thrive. Then it's time to dig a giant hole. When the two are done giving the agave a new home, they're sweaty and dusty, but Kristen always feels happy to have provided dinner for her favorite bats.

Sometimes, a farmer will even agree to have a bat box installed. Whenever that happens, Kristen comes prepared with the skills she learned for her Girl Scout project so long ago.

BORN OCTOBER 10, 1988
UNITED STATES OF AMERICA

ILLUSTRATION BY
LU ANDRADE

"IT'S NEVER TOO EARLY
TO GET STARTED. IT'S
NEVER TOO EARLY TO
GET INVOLVED. AND
THERE'S A PLACE FOR
YOU IN SCIENCE IF YOU
WANT THERE TO BE."
—KRISTEN LEAR

LAURA KOJIMA

HERPETOLOGIST

Laura sat cross-legged in front of her family's TV set and gazed, open-mouthed, at the bright, colorful images she was seeing—sprawling wet rain forests, crocodile-filled lakes, and more. At night, surrounded by her collection of stuffed animals, she dreamed of exploring those places and playing with the animals she'd seen onscreen. Her parents had immigrated to the United States from Mexico and had always encouraged her to dream big. Still, she didn't know if she could achieve her dreams. She had only ever seen people work with animals as vets or zookeepers.

Maybe I'll be a vet, she thought. But she was looking for more adventure.

When Laura grew up, she discovered the path that was right for her. She enjoyed researching reptiles and amphibians, like alligators, snakes, and salamanders, and wished other people would give them a chance. *They're gross*, some said. *They're scary*, others would chime in. But not to Laura. She'd seen them up close, touched their smooth scales and bumpy skin, and even safely removed them from homes. She knew then that she would dedicate her life to educating others about reptiles.

Today, Laura works with a team to study alligators in a lake—and she sure does get wet! Canoeing, kayaking, driving a boat, wading into the water, setting alligator traps—it's all part of the job for Laura. With just some raw chicken, she can attract any alligator to trap it for study, GPS tagging, and release. Using the data she collects, Laura can get to know her reptilian friends better and protect them for generations to come.

The little girl who spent her childhood caring for her stuffed animals grew up to study and protect the real things!

BORN AUGUST 4, 1996

MEXICO AND UNITED STATES OF AMERICA

"I AM SO FASCINATED BY THE UNKNOWN AND THE FACT THAT THERE IS SO MUCH WE WILL NEVER KNOW ABOUT."
—LAURA KOJIMA

ILLUSTRATION BY
ÁNGELA HINOJOSA

LEELA HAZZAH

CONSERVATION BIOLOGIST

Little Leela's eyes grew wide as she listened to her father tell tales about lions. When he was young, he said, their roars echoed across the desert. For years, Leela stayed up late, staring up at the stars and listening for lions, but she never heard a single growl.

Her father told her why. Lions were extinct in Egypt.

Leela was devastated. "I wanted to hear lions roaring," she despaired.

To research the powerful animals, Leela moved into a tree house in Kenya. There, she learned that a tribe called the Maasai hunted lions. It wasn't that the Maasai hated them. They actually had a deep respect for lions. Unfortunately, lions could be dangerous neighbors who attacked their cattle. Killing a lion gave a warrior a higher status in the community.

One day, a Maasai leader suggested to Leela that warriors could help in conservation efforts. They are skilled at protecting their tribe. Why not protect the lions as well? What if they were respected for how many lions they kept safe, instead of how many they killed?

Leela was thrilled to help the warriors become field biologists. She showed them how to track the animals with collars and radio equipment. Her class attracted many eager students. Even some hunters joined in the cause. Since Leela cofounded Lion Guardians, dozens of Maasai warriors have become protectors. Lion populations are recovering, and their guardians talk about new cubs like proud parents brag about their own kids. Many warriors risk their lives to protect their lions, just as they once risked their lives to hunt them.

"I know we're making a difference," Leela said. "When I first moved here, I never heard lions roaring. But now I hear lions roaring all the time."

BORN 1979

EGYPT

"AT THE END OF THE DAY, IT IS THE LOCAL PEOPLE WHO MAKE THE DECISION TO CONSERVE WILDLIFE."
—LEELA HAZZAH

ILLUSTRATION BY
RAFAELA RIJO-NÚÑEZ

MARIA DIEKMANN

CONSERVATIONIST

As a child, Maria inherited a pony from her grandmother. The spirited horse was known to misbehave. Maria spent every free moment of her day brushing his hair, riding him near her home, and talking to him with patience.

Maria would go on to travel and save animals all around the world—feeding them, nursing them back to health, and releasing them.

One day, a local businessperson in Namibia brought her an animal that would change her life: a pangolin named Roxy.

Pangolins have hundreds of scales all over their bodies. They eat millions of insects per year, and roll themselves into armored balls when they get scared. But they aren't always treated nicely and are often killed for their meat and scales. Shortly after arriving at Maria's rescue facility, Roxy did something Maria had never seen before. She climbed into Maria's lap and had a baby! The little pup, Katiti, needed help and couldn't survive on his own. Maria had been yearning for a chance to research these fascinating creatures and learn how to better protect them. Now was her chance!

For three and a half months, Maria lived with Roxy and Katiti in a small shack. No other researcher had done that before. Monitoring Katiti's birth and raising him alongside Roxy, Maria learned a lot about the shy, scaly mammals.

She has devoted her life to protecting pangolins and other endangered species, including the dwarf python and the Cape Griffon vulture. Sometimes things get hard, like when people don't see her as an environmental leader just because she's a woman. Whenever that happens, Maria simply remembers Roxy and Katiti and looks around at all she has accomplished.

BORN APRIL 27, 1965

 UNITED STATES OF AMERICA AND NAMIBIA

"IF A WOMAN FEELS STRONG ENOUGH ABOUT SOMETHING, AND SHE'S PASSIONATE ENOUGH ABOUT SOMETHING, AND SHE FINDS AN INNER STRENGTH, THEN THERE'S NOTHING THAT CAN STOP HER."
—MARIA DIEKMANN

ILLUSTRATION BY SARAH WILKINS

OLIVIA NIENABER

ENVIRONMENTALIST

Olivia loved spending her afternoons in her family's garden in Minnesota. She and her sister, Sophia, ran around in the grass, greeting the bees and spreading milkweed seeds. Milkweed plants, she learned from her mother, attract monarch butterflies in the spring and nourish them as they migrate to Mexico in the summer. The striking orange-and-black butterflies drink nectar from the flowers and lay their eggs on the leaves. The eggs hatch, and plump, busy monarch caterpillars munch on the milkweed leaves before turning into chrysalises and emerging as great winged butterflies. Olivia watched the cycle unfold in front of her eyes every year, as consistent as the seasons.

When Olivia turned 16, she had to complete a school project on ways to fight climate change. She thought and thought about a topic until it suddenly came to her—pollinators! Pollinators like bees, butterflies, and hummingbirds move pollen from flower to flower, which helps new fruits and seeds begin to grow. Without them, the planet wouldn't have food or living things. However, because of climate change, pollinators were dying. What could one teenager do to help?

Olivia had a few ideas. She planted more than 400 flowers, shrubs, and trees, and she began tending to 22 bird feeders. Soon hundreds of birds, bees, and butterflies were flitting around her family's garden, filling the air with their buzzing and chirping and fluttering wings. Feeding the caterpillars and butterflies and witnessing their return each year makes Olivia feel proud and hopeful.

Olivia continues to stand up for pollinators—her activism is in full bloom!

BORN JANUARY 18, 2003
UNITED STATES OF AMERICA

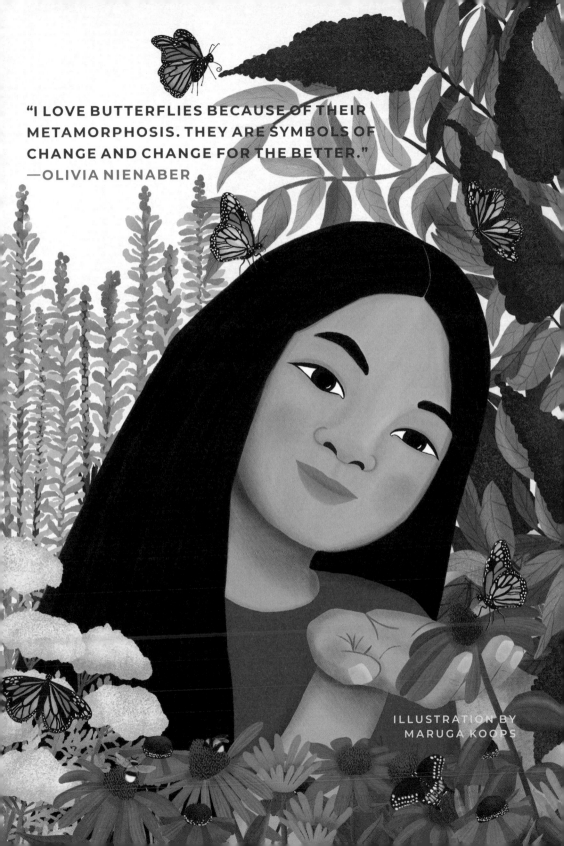

"I LOVE BUTTERFLIES BECAUSE OF THEIR METAMORPHOSIS. THEY ARE SYMBOLS OF CHANGE AND CHANGE FOR THE BETTER."
—OLIVIA NIENABER

ILLUSTRATION BY MARUGA KOOPS

RACHEL IKEMEH

CONSERVATIONIST

Rachel was doing a service project in a small town in Nigeria when she noticed trucks full of huge logs arriving every day. Where did all this wood come from?

Later, Rachel needed a job. She didn't know what she wanted to do. So she applied for every job she saw. When she became an intern at the Nigerian Conservation Foundation, she'd never even been to a zoo before!

One day, Rachel and the other interns met a renowned conservationist for a lesson on the threats to animals in Africa. As Rachel listened to him talk about the dangers of hunting, she realized something. *He's wrong.* At first, Rachel didn't say anything. She tried to push the image of those trucks full of logs out of her mind. But finally, she knew she had to speak up.

"No, it's not hunting," she said. "It's habitat loss."

Looking back at it now, Rachel laughs. "I was arguing with this expert with so many years of experience," she says. But she knew what she had seen.

The conservationist appreciated her spunk and became her mentor, helping Rachel on her new mission: to combat habitat loss across Nigeria. Today, Rachel runs the SW/Niger Delta Forest Project, which protects animals like the extremely endangered Niger Delta red colobus. These rare monkeys do not have thumbs. They eat leaves and spend their time high up in the canopies of trees. As the population of the red colobus dwindled to about 500, Rachel and her team got to work. They spread the word and encouraged local communities to protect their trees and preserve the delicate ecosystem that supported the red colobus. Because of Rachel, these crimson creatures are getting the attention they need to prosper.

BIRTH DATE UNKNOWN
NIGERIA

ILLUSTRATION BY
RAE CRAWFORD

"THE GREATEST
OPTIMISM I'VE
SEEN REALLY IS
IN PEOPLE, AND
I THINK PEOPLE
REALLY HAVE
THE CAPACITY TO
BE THE BIGGEST
CHAMPIONS FOR
CONSERVATION."
—RACHEL IKEMEH

SAENGDUEAN "LEK" CHAILERT

ANIMAL RIGHTS ACTIVIST

Once there was a girl who had pigs for brothers and a gibbon for a sister. From her earliest memories, Lek has considered animals her family. She grew up with chickens, dogs, and any other critter her grandfather found caught in a trap in the jungle. Lek saw the fear and confusion in the eyes of those injured animals, and she did everything she could to help them feel comfortable. Lek and her grandfather gave them food and medicine, and Lek sometimes snuck her favorite rescues into her bed at night to cuddle.

One day, Lek heard an exhausted cry. She found an old bull elephant being forced to drag a huge log up a steep hill. Lek had heard that sound for years, but she hadn't known what it was. Now, it haunted her.

Lek immediately bought a book on tending to animal injuries. She took medicine back to the elephant she'd seen and helped his keepers care for him. They told her about another sick elephant they knew, so she helped that one too. And then another . . . and then another.

The people Lek met told her they didn't know what to do with old, sick, or injured animals. Lek heard her calling as loud and clear as the elephant's cries. She started a reserve—somewhere elephants could live in peace, washing themselves in the river and eating bananas out of visitors' hands.

Lek employs hundreds of people to care for more than 5,000 animals of all kinds. Some of the residents of her Elephant Nature Park are wildlife who just need a quick vet visit. Others are creatures that need a place to live out their days. Lek says she can still read the fear in their eyes when they first come to her, but eventually all of them learn that they're family.

BORN OCTOBER 6, 1961
THAILAND

ILLUSTRATION BY
AVANI DWIVEDI

"WE
UNDERSTAND,
EVEN IF WE
SPEAK A
DIFFERENT
LANGUAGE.
BUT WE
UNDERSTAND
EACH OTHER."
—SAENGDUEAN
"LEK" CHAILERT

SAMI BAYLY

Once there was a girl who saw the beauty in every animal. Sami and her family lived in a house full of pets—dogs, guinea pigs, rabbits, fish, birds, miniature ponies, cows, and donkeys!

Young Sami and her artist mom painted them all.

Sami's mom created larger-than-life portraits, while Sami struggled to come up with good outlines of her furry and scaly friends. But she didn't let herself get discouraged. Sami would look up at walls filled with her mother's paintings and think, *Mine will look like that one day too*. She dove in, drawing and painting for years and even studying art in college.

Later, Sami caught herself rolling her eyes at the way people made fun of the Australian white ibis. These birds steal crusts of bread, leftover french fries, and other waste out of garbage cans, earning themselves the nickname "bin chicken." Many Australians think they're a bit of a nuisance. Not Sami.

She decided to put her years of artistic practice into showing people how majestic this troublesome ibis truly was. Sami gathered her paints, brushes, and a large sheet of watercolor paper. She painted carefully, laying down layer after layer of color to build a detailed portrait of a bin chicken's dark, curved beak and feathery white body.

Sami had hoped to simply change a few people's minds about the ibis. But her painting went viral, and Sami found herself with a book deal!

Readers can't get enough of her portraits of peculiar animals. Sami's paintings don't look like her mom's. Her art style is all her own, so intricate and fun. And it's making people around the world look at "ugly" or "unusual" animals in a whole new way.

BORN FEBRUARY 13, 1996

AUSTRALIA

ILLUSTRATION BY
SAMI BAYLY

"WHO ARE HUMANS TO
JUDGE AN ANIMAL BASED
ON ITS APPEARANCE?"
—SAMI BAYLY

SUE CHIN

ARCHITECT

When Sue was 12 years old, she and her family moved from London to New York. The Bronx Zoo quickly became her favorite place in her new neighborhood. Every weekend, she'd watch the tigers pacing through the tall grass and the elephants rolling around in the dirt.

As a teenager, she even started working at the zoo. A job selling hot dogs led her to her dream job! While studying architecture in college, she taught zoo guests about conservation. She started to wonder if there was a way to combine her love of design with her love of animals.

One day, she spotted a listing for a job that stopped her in her tracks: exhibit designer. Of course! Just like a house is important to keeping people happy and healthy, an animal's habitat in a zoo is important to keeping *it* happy and healthy. And seeing an animal in a copy of its natural environment helps zoo visitors understand it better.

Now Sue travels the world looking for exactly the right way to make cozy dwellings for the clever monkeys, trumpeting elephants, and other amazing creatures that live in New York zoos. Do their cousins in the wild like to splash in swamps or sunbathe in the sand? Do they snooze in caves or curl up in tall trees? Whatever it is, Sue can build it.

At the Bronx Zoo's Tiger Mountain, Sue re-created an enormous leafy green Siberian forest. There, tigers can lounge on heated boulders and splash in a lake. Through tall windows, guests can see the tigers' bold orange-and-black stripes up close as the big cats cool off in their "kitty pool."

Sue and her colleagues bring mud huts, alpine slopes, African savannas, rain forests, and other habitats to zoos, so animals can feel at home.

BIRTH DATE UNKNOWN
UNITED KINGDOM AND UNITED STATES OF AMERICA

ILLUSTRATION BY
JIALEI SUN

"DESIGN AND
WILDLIFE ARE MY
PASSIONS."
—SUE CHIN

TEMPLE GRANDIN

PROFESSOR OF ANIMAL SCIENCES

SCAN TO HEAR MORE!

From the time Temple was very young, she knew she was different. She has autism, which means her brain works differently from other people's. Temple didn't begin to speak until she was nearly four years old. It wasn't easy for her to make friends, and people weren't always nice to her. Temple just wanted to find somewhere she belonged.

When she was 14, Temple got her wish. Her family sent her to a school with other kids with autism. It was a special school on a farm with horses, dairy cows, and lots of grass to play around in.

There, Temple thrived. The hands-on chores of the farm made sense to her, and she began to feel connected to the animals. One day, she decided to explore the horse stables. At first, she was overwhelmed by the smells of hay and manure and the horses' loud whinnies and snorts. But the moment she saw them—with their strong bodies, dewy eyes, and long manes—she fell in love.

Temple went horseback riding almost every day. She even got a job at school taking care of the horses. She brushed them, fed them, and took them out to pasture. Tending to the horses boosted Temple's confidence and connected her with friends who also loved animals. She knew she had found her calling.

When she grew up, Temple built her career around educating people about autism and improving the treatment of farm animals.

"The world needs all types of minds," Temple says.

Through her speeches, books, and inventions, Temple uses her brilliant brain to inspire people to be kinder to all living things.

BORN AUGUST 29, 1947
UNITED STATES OF AMERICA

"NATURE IS CRUEL, BUT
WE DON'T HAVE TO BE."
—TEMPLE GRANDIN

ILLUSTRATION BY
JANIE SECKER

TOLANI FRANCISCO

VETERINARIAN

Once there was a girl named Tolani. On her tribe's reservation in New Mexico, her great-grandfather raised cattle, sheep, and horses. So did her grandfathers and her father, like many of her Laguna ancestors. Running around outside, Tolani saved every creature she found, nursing them to health before letting them go free. One day, when she was 15 years old, she saw a sheep horribly injured while getting shorn. There was nothing she could do to help the poor animal. From that moment on, she knew something important about her future: she'd be a veterinarian.

At veterinary school, Tolani took a different route from many of her classmates. Sure, she loved cats and dogs. But she also loved cows. And she wasn't afraid to look after big animals, like horses, and endangered bison and elk. Bison and elk are mighty creatures. They can weigh as much as pickup trucks! But they can still benefit from frequent checkups, just like pets and people do. And that's where Tolani comes in.

Tolani's calling has taken her around the world. She has spent time caring for bison and elk in Yellowstone National Park—looking into their mouths, listening to their hearts, lungs, and stomachs with a stethoscope, and taking their temperatures. She's treated elk in the Jicarilla Apache Nation, and battled foot-and-mouth disease in cattle and sheep in Bolivia and the United Kingdom. And now she works to protect and manage wild horses and burros as part of the US Forest Service.

Tolani founded an animal hospital on her reservation, where she tends to a population that is often overlooked: reservation animals. She knows her work doesn't just help the four-legged creatures. It helps the two-legged ones too!

BORN MAY 10, 1965

UNITED STATES OF AMERICA

ILLUSTRATION BY
ANGELA ACEVEDO PEREZ

"RESERVATION ANIMALS STILL DESERVE THE SAME QUALITY CARE AS THOSE LIVING IN MORE PROSPEROUS AREAS. WE OWE THAT MUCH TO OUR FOUR-LEGGED BROTHERS AND SISTERS."
—TOLANI FRANCISCO

WRITE YOUR STORY

DRAW YOUR PORTRAIT

BE AN ANIMAL ALLY

These activities were designed by Bindi Irwin and her team of Wildlife Warriors to help you learn even more about conservation and what it means to be an animal ally.

✦ **DON'T TRASH IT, COMPOST IT!**

Building your own composter is a great way to reuse and recycle. You can compost lots of food and household waste that you might normally throw out, like banana peels, coffee grounds, apple cores, eggshells, tea bags, fallen leaves, and shredded newspaper. Here's how:

- Grab a plastic container with a lid. If you have a backyard, balcony, or patio, you can put your compost bin outside. (If you live in a city, store your compost in your freezer so it doesn't stink up the kitchen before you take it to a compost collection site.)
- Fill up your container. Make sure to chop up larger food waste into smaller pieces.
- When your container is full, you can use your compost to feed your garden or houseplants, or bring it to a local farmer's market that collects compost.

The last step? Feel good about saving valuable household waste!

✦ **BUILD A BIRD'S NEST**

Want to get a taste of building animal habitats like Sue Chin? Make a bird's nest.

- Grab a clean ice cream or yogurt container and use a pen to poke holes in the bottom so rainwater can drain out.
- Fill your container with dry grass and leaves to create a soft base.
- Have your grown-up help you find a tree branch to fasten your nest to. Placing it high above the ground will keep it safe from predators. Monitor your nest to see if a chirping, feathered family moves in!

⟡ MAKE A LOUNGE FOR LITTLE CRITTERS

Christina Gorsuch had to learn all about how different animals live and interact with their environments to keep them happy and healthy. This next activity invites you to practice building an environment where lizards or insects might thrive.

- Gather rocks, pipes, hollow logs, or an old ceramic or terra-cotta pot.
- Choose a warm and sunny place and arrange and stack these items together to make lots of nooks and crannies for lizards and insects to hide in. These hiding places will keep them safe from predators and wet weather.
- Lizards love to eat seeds, berries, and insects. Add plants that produce seeds or berries as an extra lizard treat! These plants will also attract insects that the lizards eat. If you do not live in a place with lots of lizards, do some research about local butterflies and insects and plant what they like to nibble on.
- A shallow, hidden water bowl is great for little critters too.

⟡ MAKE A RESCUE KIT

Saengduean "Lek" Chailert grew up with many rescued animals, so she learned quickly how to treat injuries. As animals try to live among us in our bustling cities and towns, you might come across an animal who needs help too. Here's how to make an animal rescue kit so you'll always be prepared:

- Get a cardboard box or tote bag and label it "Animal Rescue Kit."
- The first thing to do when you see an injured animal is to call in the professionals. So write down the name and number of a local veterinarian or animal hospital that treats wild animals. Keep it at the very top of your rescue kit.
- Next, grab the following supplies: a flashlight, a pair of thick gloves, a towel, and a highly visible vest. These will come in handy when help arrives.

RESEARCH AND REPORT

Learning about the endangered animals in your own area is an excellent way to discover how to protect them.

- With a grown-up, look up a list of endangered species in your state or region. Pick the one that interests you most.
- Go online or peruse nonfiction books. Find out as much as you can about that animal. What do they eat? Where do they live? Which animals are their predators? Do they live by themselves or in groups?
- Next, find out why they are endangered. Perhaps they are a marine animal that is overfished. Or maybe hunting is contributing to population loss.

Now it's time to present your findings! Write an article, create a slideshow, or make a poster about the animal you researched and the facts you discovered. Share your project with your local paper or school group.

ABOUT WILDLIFE WARRIORS

Wildlife Warriors was established in 2002 by Steve and Terri Irwin as a way to include and involve other caring people in the protection of injured, threatened, or endangered wildlife—from the individual animal to an entire species. Today, with 11 global conservation projects, from protecting tigers in Sumatra to crocodiles on the Steve Irwin Wildlife Reserve, Wildlife Warriors is continuing Steve's legacy.

Wildlife Warriors' flagship project, the Australia Zoo Wildlife Hospital, is one of the largest and busiest of its kind in the world, having treated more than 110,000 animals since opening its doors in 2004. Australia Zoo and Wildlife Warriors also proudly protect more than 450,000 acres (703 square miles) of habitat dedicated solely to the research and conservation of wildlife and wild places throughout Queensland, Australia.

Visionary Wildlife Warriors, a youth ambassador program, is inspiring the next generation to conserve the natural world. The program offers young people ages 4 to 17 around the world the opportunity to grow their knowledge, raise funds, take part in conservation missions in their local communities, and nominate others for the coveted yearly Visionary Wildlife Warrior Award.

To find out more, visit www.wildlifewarriors.org.au.

SKETCH AND SHARE

Are you an animal lover? Do you like to draw? Carry a sketch pad and some colored pencils with you wherever you go so you can sketch any cats you come across, birds you spot at the park, or squirrels you see scampering across the grass. To celebrate the furry friends that keep the folks at Rebel Girls smiling, designer and illustrator Kristen Brittain sketched a bunch of beloved Rebel Girls' pets. Meet them all!

Do you have an animal drawing you'd like to show off? Send us an email at editorial@rebelgirls.com. From time to time, we'll share the artwork of animal allies like you.

MORE STORIES!

For more stories about amazing women and girls, check out other Rebel Girls books.

LISTEN TO MORE EMPOWERING STORIES ON THE REBEL GIRLS APP!

Download the app to listen to beloved Rebel Girls stories as well as brand-new tales of extraordinary women. Filled with the adventures and accomplishments of women from around the world and throughout history, the Rebel Girls app is designed to entertain, inspire, and build confidence in listeners everywhere.

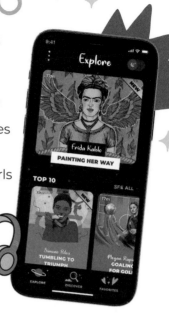

THE ILLUSTRATORS

Twenty-five extraordinary female artists from all over the world illustrated the portraits in this book.

ANGELA ACEVEDO PEREZ, PERU, 55

ÁNGELA HINOJOSA, MEXICO, 37

AVANI DWIVEDI, INDIA, 47

BARBARA DZIADOSZ, GERMANY, 21

DÉBORA ISLAS, BRAZIL, 17

EMMA PEDERSEN, CANADA, 9

EMMANUELLE WALKER, CANADA, 29

IZZY EVANS, UK, 15

JANIE SECKER, NEW ZEALAND, 53

JIALEI SUN, US, 51

JOANNE DERTILI, GREECE, 11

JOJO CLINCH, UK, 7

JUNE TIEN, VIETNAM, 25

KRISTEN BRITTAIN, US, 33, 61

LAURA PROIETTI, ITALY, 13

LEIRE SALABERRIA, SPAIN, 27

LU ANDRADE, ECUADOR, 35

MARUGA KOOPS, THE NETHERLANDS, 43

MONIQUE STEELE, US, 23

NATALIA CARDONA PUERTA, US, 19

RAE CRAWFORD, US, 45

RAFAELA RIJO-NÚÑEZ, GERMANY, 39

SAMI BAYLY, AUSTRALIA, 49

SARAH WILKINS, NEW ZEALAND, 41

SHIANE SALABIE, JAMAICA, 31

ABOUT REBEL GIRLS

REBEL GIRLS is a global, multi-platform empowerment brand dedicated to helping raise the most inspired and confident generation of girls through content, experiences, products, and community. Originating from an international best-selling children's book, Rebel Girls amplifies stories of real-life women throughout history, geography, and field of excellence. With a growing community of nearly 20 million self-identified Rebel Girls spanning more than 100 countries, the brand engages with Generation Alpha through its book series, award-winning podcast, events, and merchandise. With the 2021 launch of the Rebel Girls app, the company has created a flagship destination for girls to explore a wondrous world filled with inspiring true stories of extraordinary women.

Join the Rebel Girls community:

- Facebook: facebook.com/rebelgirls
- Instagram: @rebelgirls
- Twitter: @rebelgirlsbook
- TikTok: @rebelgirlsbook
- Web: rebelgirls.com
- Podcast: rebelgirls.com/podcast
- App: rebelgirls.com/app

If you liked this book, please take a moment to review it wherever you prefer!